HOW TO BE A

Jackie Robb

HAMLYN

Acknowledgements
Design: Robert Mathias, Publishing Workshop
Illustrations: Marilyn Day
Photography: Chris King

All photographs other than those credited below were
specially taken for this book by Chris King.

Clothing and equipment for photography
kindly supplied by
ISI Sportswear and Arena UK

All Sport Photographic/Trevor Jones 25, Steve
Powell 25; Associated Sports Photography front
jacket, 23; The Dance Library/Darryl Williams 28-29
(three top pictures); Tim Hughes 20; Picture Bank
Photo Library 21, 45 (centre), 58; Rex Features 16,
24, front jacket; Sporting Pictures (UK) 35, 50; Dave
Spurdens 20-21; Syndication International/Woman's
Own 46; Judy Todd 27.
Photography on page 45 (top right) by kind
permission of Black beauty & hair magazine,
photographer Carl Max.
Photograph on page 45 (top left) by courtesy of
Jingles International.

Published 1985 by
Hamlyn Publishing
A division of The Hamlyn Publishing Group Limited,
Bridge House, London Road, Twickenham, Middlesex,
England.

Printed in Italy
ISBN 0 600 30913 4

CONTENTS

GET SUPER FIT!

These days everybody realises that keeping fit is vital if we want to make the most of a busy life. Health isn't just something that concerns doctors and nurses, but it's something we all ought to be interested in, for our own good. We're all responsible for our *own* fitness and well-being.

If you want to be super-fit you have to treat your body super-well! So how do you do the very best for your body? Well, imagine your body is a finely-tuned engine . . . It needs the right kind of fuel (wholesome food), a little care and attention to the bodywork and, last but definitely not least, it needs to be kept moving!

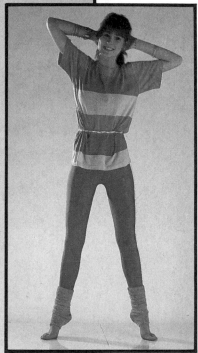

EXERCISE FOR ENERGY

Taking up some form of exercise is a great way to get fit *and* have fun while you're about it. Whether you're aiming to be a winner on the sports field, or a whizz on the dance-floor – or you simply want to be supple and energy-packed – it's a good idea to get moving and try a daily exercise session.

It's best to set aside a certain time each day for exercising – ideally first thing in the morning if you have the time before school. Exercise peps you up and gets everything (even a sleepy brain) ticking over nicely.

Always make sure you exercise where there's plenty of room – in Summer the garden is a great place to try your keep-fit routine. It's best to exercise on a soft floor with a little 'give' – a carpeted wood floor is ideal, but for safety's sake never exercise on a highly polished floor with loose rugs. Remember exercise should be fun, so don't push yourself too hard. Forget all that stuff about going for 'the burn', and just enjoy yourself!

... stamina, strength, suppleness and shape! These are the four s's that regular exercise can give you. You need stamina to keep going in many competitive sports (and throughout busy days!) . . . You need to be supple if you want to dance and move well, or simply keep your body as flexible as Nature intended . . . You need strength to see you through tough jobs, and to give you the muscle power for sports and athletics . . . And you want a trim shape because it helps you feel good about yourself, and it

SUPER S STANDS FOR...

makes you look good too!

Taking regular exercise is the best way of keeping the flab at bay because exercise uses up the energy from the food you eat, and makes sure that second helping doesn't end up as extra inches on your waist! So, if you want to stay in trim, it helps if you keep on the move. Even everyday exercise can help burn calories and firm your figure. Walking is one of the best exercises there is for the whole body – if you fit in a walk of twenty minutes or so every day you'll be building up

you're getting warmer!

1.HEAD ROLLS
Stand up straight, arms by your sides, feet apart. Let your head drop back gently, then roll it to the left, the front, then to the right for the slow count of 10. Repeat 5 times to the left and 5 to the right.

2. ARM SWINGS
Stand with feet apart, arms out straight in front of the chest, palms touching. Raise the arms above the head, then lower them to the sides pushing the arms back slightly at the same time.

your stamina and you'll feel brighter. It's a good idea to avoid taking a bus for short journeys and to take a brisk walk instead! Many of the ordinary movements you do every day are good for keeping you in shape and helping you stay super-fit. Climbing stairs, for instance, helps tone the leg muscles and keeps your seat neat. Even helping with the housework can keep you supple as you bend and stretch. Stay active, and you'll keep the 'puppy-fat' at bay and feel and look lively too.

What's Aerobic Exercise?

Aerobic exercise is vigorous, rhythmic exercise that makes you breathe more rapidly, and keeps you breathing fast for a length of time. Although folk seem to think there's something new about aerobics, in fact a lot of everyday exercises can be called aerobic if they're done in the right way – running, brisk walking, vigorous dancing, and cycling are among the many aerobic activities you can do.

The following exercises are the perfect limbering movements for any exercise or sports session. They warm up the muscles, help loosen up joints, and make sure you feel raring to go!

3. TRUNK TWISTERS
Stand with feet apart, arms out straight in front. Now swing the right arm around to the right as far as it will go, keeping your eyes on the moving hand. Return to starting position and repeat to the left side. Do 5 repetitions each side, alternately.

4. KNEES UP
Stand with your feet together, then bring one knee up to your chest, pulling it with your hands. Then let your head fall forward to touch your knee with your forehead. Repeat with the other leg. Try 5 repetitions each side.

SHAPE UP

The following exercises, done on a daily basis, will help you keep fit and in good shape. But remember, go gently to begin with – if any movement seems hard at first do fewer repetitions, and slowly work up to more. Take it easy but persevere, and you'll soon shape up . . .

1 SPLIT JUMPS Stand with feet together, arms at your sides, then jump, moving the feet apart, and raising your arms above your head to clap the palms together. Jump back to the starting position and repeating 10–15 times.

2 PUNCH & JOG

Try some jogging on the spot. As you raise the right knee, punch out the left hand and, as you raise the left knee, punch out the right fist. You'll soon get a rhythm going. Aim to raise each knee 10 times.

3 LEG RAISES

Lie on your right side, supporting your head with your right hand. Raise the left leg, moving it slightly behind the line of the body. Lower it to the starting position and raise again. Repeat 5–10 times with each leg.

4. DOG KICKS

Kneel down on all fours, and bend one knee up underneath you, while lowering the head. Then, raising the head to look at the ceiling kick the leg out to the back. Repeat 10 times with each leg.

5. HEEL'N TOE TAPPERS

Lie on your back on the floor, arms out-stretched by your sides. Bend your legs up and place the soles of the feet together. Then bring the knees together feet apart, before returning to the soles together position. Repeat 5 times.

6. PUPPET BENDS

Stand up straight, arms by your sides, palms against upper thighs. Now bend to the right letting the right arm slide down the right leg, as far as you can comfortably go Return to starting position and repeat 5 times each side.

7. HIP ROLLS

Lie on the floor, arms outstretched. Keeping your knees together, bend your legs up, so that the body forms a Z shape. Now, still keeping the knees together, roll the knees over to almost touch the ground at the left hand side. Roll back through the starting position to the right side. Do the entire movement 5 times.

8. ARM CIRCLES

Stand up straight, arms out to the sides, holding a tennis ball, apple or orange tightly in each hand. Keeping the arms straight, circle them simultaneously backwards to the count of 20, then circle them forwards to the count of 20.

You don't have to be a would-be slimmer to benefit from regular exercise. Even those who'd like to gain a little weight – or put on an inch or two in strategic places – can shape up thanks to exercise. It's worth noting that the actors who played Superman and Supergirl both built their bodies up for their super-roles with special exercises.

Generally, those who want to add shapely muscle should do exercises (like the ones on pages 12–15) slower than the fatties who want to lose some weight really aiming to feel the muscles working as they move.

For would-be super girls who simply want to strengthen their legs for their favourite sport (or shape up calves and thighs) the following two exercises are well worth a try.

The Heel Raise

Place a large book (an encyclopedia or phone book) on the floor. Stand on it so that your heels overlap it at the back. Now raise onto tiptoes, feeling the muscles pulling, and lower, so that the heels *nearly* touch the floor. Repeat slowly 8 times. To strengthen and shape the whole lower leg you can try the same movement with toes turned out, or in, as well.

The Thigh Trembler

Stand up straight with your back against a wall, then slowly slide down the wall until you are in a 'sitting' position (but sitting on thin air!) with your thighs straight out in front of you, and your legs forming a right angle shape. Hold as long as you comfortably can. (You'll find you'll be able to hold for longer periods as your muscles begin to strengthen.)

SKINNY KID TO SUPER KID

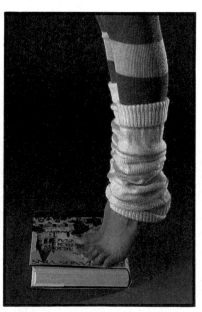

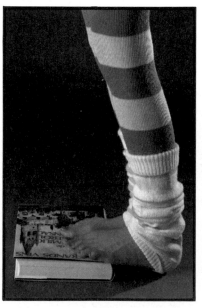

your keep fit kit

You don't have to spend a fortune on exercise-wear. Your school games kit or a set of cotton underwear is perfect for everyday exercising. If you want to really feel the part when you're doing your bend 'n' stretch routine, though, you may like to wear a leotard which moves with you, or a tracksuit which allows freedom of movement. You may like to wear leg warmers too – these have a practical purpose in that they warm up the muscles and help avoid strain during hectic exercise sessions.

If you want to put your best foot forward when you're exercising you may want to wear training shoes – these are good for lengthy jogging sessions or any

SKIP IT!

Skipping is a great exercise for everyone – it works the leg and arm muscles and gets you breathing faster. Those who know the ropes wear trainers and comfy clothes when skipping through an exercise session.

bouncy exercise since the shaped heels absorb the shock of all that pounding. Ordinary flat-heeled gym shoes or bare feet (depending on the floor) are okay for

short, gentle keep-fit sessions. Make sure you wear absorbent cotton socks if you do wear trainers or gym shoes – these will help to prevent perspiration problems. Footwear is very important for sporty types – when you're kitting yourself out for any type of exercise, think about your feet first, and you'll get off on the right footing!

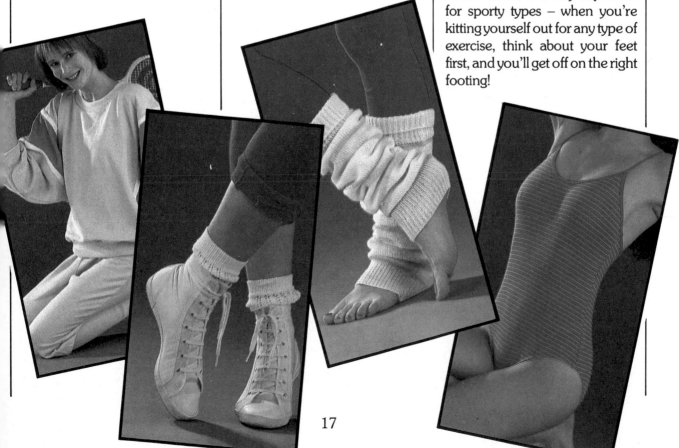

STAND UP

Picture Superman with round shoulders . . . Imagine a concave-chested Supergirl slouching around . . . Can't do it, can you? Because the fact is dynamic folk always stand up to the world and walk tall. The way you move, stand and sit affects, and reflects, the way you feel – folk who are miserable tend to hunch over. If you stand or sit like this for long periods you could end up feeling pretty low too!

Doctors now say that good posture – holding yourself straight and tall – actually helps you feel more lively, and improves your brain-power in the long run. One thing's for sure, it certainly improves the way you look.

Good posture doesn't mean standing around with a ramrod spine, looking as if you've left the coathanger in your jacket! It simply means standing so that the body's muscles and internal organs can work properly. If you're standing and moving correctly your shoulders will be comfortably low (not hunched up or sagging forward), your back will be straight (not arched or bending forwards). To get used to what good posture feels like it helps to try bad posture – hunch your shoulders and let yourself sag forwards from the waist. Now ease your shoulders back and straighten up and see how good it feels. There's a standard exercise you can try to get used to the feel of a proper stance. Just lift your arms above your head, and lift your shoulders up with them as if you're reaching for the ceiling and trying to stretch your spine from the waist. Then lower your arms and relax, dropping your shoulders down, and allowing them to go slightly back. Memorise that feeling, if you want to stand tall.

FOR YOURSELF

Reach for the sky after each exercise session, and improve your posture!

SAFETY FIRST

To feel good after an exercise session, follow these rules for safe exercising:

1. Always cool down after exercising – do lots of stretching movements to tail off your session the gentle way.
2. Don't have a hot bath or shower immediately afterwards – go for a warm wash-down instead.
3. **Never** push yourself to do any exercise if it hurts.
4. Make sure you never hold your breath when you exercise – breathe normally to prevent dizziness.
5. Don't run on your toes when jogging on the spot – the heels should touch the ground to prevent muscle damage.
6. Don't exercise after a heavy meal.
7. Don't exercise in a stuffy atmosphere.
8. Avoid doing any exercise which asks you to bend forwards with your legs straight (toe-touching, for instance). Always bend the knees slightly.
9. Never exercise if you have a cold or are feeling weak.
10. Don't got in for any lengthy bouncing exercise on a hard concrete or tiled floor.

Walk this Way!

Walking with your head up and shoulders down and slightly back gives your lungs the room to work, and makes you look more trim too. You should walk with your feet parallel, toes pointing straight ahead, so that your weight is distributed evenly over your feet. Walking properly – taking rhythmic steps, and letting your arms swing naturally – is a very good exercise in itself!

Sit Up!

You can even do your body some good while you sit still. When you sit you should try to keep your feet firmly planted on the floor, legs slightly apart, and the weight of your body resting evenly on your buttocks. This is a good way to sit for long periods at a desk, or while watching television if you don't want to get that tired, achey feeling.

If you want occasionally to cross your legs, try to cross them at the ankle only. If you cross them further up your body isn't properly balanced. If you're reading it is also a good idea to lift your book up to face level, rather than hunch over it. This puts much less strain on the neck and means you'll feel alert for longer.

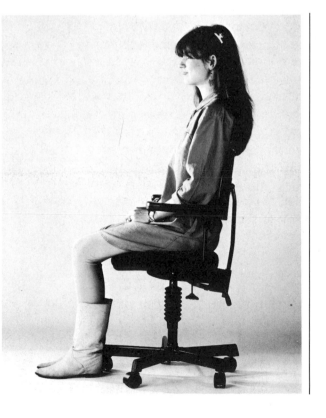

BE A SPORT

Whether you see yourself as a budding athlete or not, taking up a sport is certainly a lot of fun, and one of the best ways of beating that old school holiday/weekend boredom.

You don't have to be a medal or trophy-winner to get a lot out of being involved in a sport: apart from the obvious enjoyment, being sporty can improve your general fitness and really help you feel like a super kid. In short, when it comes to taking part in sporty activities, everyone's a winner!

On Your Bike!
Ever since those three letters BMX became an everyday part of our language, cycling has been *the* popular sport among the under-16s. BMX, of course, is the latest exhilarating cycle sport which combines all the thrills and spills of motorcycle Motorcross with the safer aspects of cycling. Obviously for this you need a specially adapted, sturdy but light cycle – a BMX bike – and helmet and protective clothing to avoid painful scrapes when the 'wheelies' and other stunts don't quite work out! You should go for a helmet that is strong (not the lightweight type with

holes), and as close as possible to the type used in motorbike racing. It's vitally important to get the right size, so try on lots of helmets, and ask advice in the shops.

Of course when you first get a BMX bike you won't be able to attempt all the stunts you see on the television. You've got to learn to control the bike properly before you even attempt any fancy stuff! It goes without saying of course that you can't do BMX stunts in the streets – instead

find out where there is a track or spare ground that you can safely use near your own home.

Fun on Wheels
Of course BMX is just one of the ways you can get fit, and have fun, on your bike. Cycling is one of the best aerobic exercises there is, building up the strength of your heart and lungs. It also strengthens the leg muscles, which means it can help you get in training for other sports that require a lot of leg work.

20

Is it a girl, is it a plane? . . . No, it's super girl on BMX wheels! (But it takes a lot of training to do stunts like these!)

Obviously you can't ride your bike in the streets among traffic until you know the rules of the road. Until then it's best to stick to cycle tracks – enquire if there are any tracks in local parks, so you can enjoy cycling without any risks.

Once you are ready to take to the roads always remember to give clear hand signals, and to wear light reflective clothing on dark days. For safety's sake you should never ride a bike that's too big for you, and you should always keep your bike in good shape. When you're growing be sure that you adjust your bike to fit you; you should be able to rest the balls of your feet on the floor, and bend your legs slightly when you're sitting comfortably in the saddle.

Cycling is good fun for all the family so you might want to persuade Mum and Dad to get on their bikes and join you for a country run. You could become a super-fit family in no time!

IN THE SWIM

As well as keeping you fit, swimming keeps you supple – the weight of the water supports your body, so your joints can move more freely.

Swimming is the ideal sport for those who are a little chubbier than they'd like to be. It's the one sport where your weight isn't necessarily a disadvantage, because the water is bearing the extra poundage and it's also an excellent body toner for fatties who want to shape up.

Improving Fitness at a Stroke

To be sure you get all the benefits possible out of swimming you should use different strokes – the breast stroke, for instance, exercises the arm and chest muscles and also the hips and knees. The back-stroke and crawl exercise the shoulders, abdomen and buttocks. Obviously you can't hope to do all the strokes if you're still a learner swimmer, but if you take lessons at a local pool you'll gradually work up to the more difficult strokes. It's always best to take lessons from a qualified teacher – if you simply try to teach yourself to swim, or if you rely on another member of the family for lessons, you might not be

It's generally agreed that swimming is one of the best exercises there is for toning the muscles and developing strength and stamina. When you swim you give every part of your body a workout.

able to learn all the breathing, diving, and energy-saving (or life-saving) techniques that could give extra power to your stroke.

A Safer Splash

There are certain rules to obey if you want to swim safely – for instance you shouldn't swim within 2 hours of a heavy meal (although with a light meal of, say, a sandwich there shouldn't be any problem). You shouldn't let yourself get too cold or you could get cramp which can be very dangerous in deep water. You should never stay in cool water for long periods – if you feel chilly or shivery and your lips turn blue-ish it's time to head for the towel!

You should never get out of your depth, or swim where there are dangerous currents or tides. It's also a good idea to avoid swimming if you have a heavy cold or any skin irritation. Observe these rules and you'll be able to splash out safely.

Getting Equipped . . .

If you find you are always screwing up your eyes, or pool or sea water seems to irritate them, goggles are a good piece of safety equipment to buy. You must shop around for goggles carefully though – make sure they are well-cushioned and not too tight. Tight goggles may apply too much pressure around the eye. It isn't a good idea to borrow goggles because what fits one person perfectly may not be right for someone else. Make sure, too, that your goggles are shatterproof. It's also worth remembering that you should be very careful when removing your goggles – always slide them upwards over the head and *don't* pull them out in front of the eyes where they can rebound and hurt you.

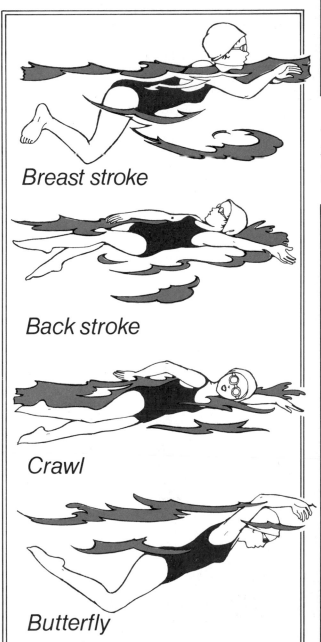

Breast stroke

Back stroke

Crawl

Butterfly

Top: *Sarah Hardcastle, Bronze Medal winner in 800m freestyle 1984 Olympic Games. Below: Caroline Holmyard and Carolyn Wilson, synchronized swimmers in the 1984 Olympic Games*

get your skates on!

Skating is a very graceful sport – but it also requires a lot of muscle power. Even if you have no hopes of reaching competition standard, skating can be good for you. It strengthens the muscles, helps you develop good co-ordination (something which is important in every sport) and strengthens weak ankles. It also helps you develop good balance and awareness of your body, so you'll be a graceful mover *off* the ice too.

If you'd like to take up skating – even just for fun – it is always worth having beginners' lessons. Professional tuition will help you overcome any fear of the ice, and get you over the 'wobblies'! After beginners' lessons you won't be able to do fancy leaps and turns, but you will be able to enjoy yourself on the ice. You'll be able to skate backwards and forwards and stop safely. Your teacher will explain how a skate moves,

Torvil and Dean, Gold Medal ice dance champions in the 1984 Olympic Games

and exactly how it propels you forward – it isn't as easy as simply walking on ice, but it's great fun when you've got the hang of it.

Ballet can be good training for ice skating, and roller skating can help too. Although the feel of roller skates and ice skates *is* very different, roller skating teaches you balance and gives you the idea of movement. Most skaters say that ice skating is actually easier than roller skating.

Get Equipped . . .

Although many girls may be tempted to buy the frilly-skirted dresses professional skaters wear, for beginners, or any skater in training, a tracksuit is really the most practical outfit. It is very cold in an ice rink, and your clothes should be geared to the low temperature. Beginners who take a tumble in a short skirt and thin tights will soon feel miserable and uncomfortable.

When you first start learning to skate you'll probably hire boots – remember to choose a pair that feels comfortable and allows you to move easily. Don't just go for your usual shoe size without trying others, as sizes can vary. If possible it is best to buy your own boots once you're sure you are going to skate regularly. Your own boots will mould to the individual shape of your foot over a period of time (that's why it isn't always a good idea to buy second-hand boots, because your feet will have to fit into someone else's 'mould').

If you are buying boots go for the cheapest type that is the right fit for you – buying expensive ones and hoping to grow into them, and make them last, is *not* a good idea.

25

IN THE RUNNING

Running is one of the most popular sports right now – for all ages. You don't have to have ambitions to be a marathon runner either to get the benefits. There are organised 'fun runs' all over the world now for those who just run for the sheer joy of it.

Running is one of the best ways of getting and staying fit (it's an aerobic exercise, so is good for your general health), and is excellent training for other sports such as tennis, badminton and squash and team games such as football, netball, rounders, volleyball and hockey.

It goes without saying that you should take things easily and shouldn't try to get in on the mini-marathon circuit too early. You shouldn't try to run before you can walk for ten minutes or so at a brisk pace without feeling at all out of breath. One good way of getting fit for running is to go in for 'jalking' – a cross between brisk walking and jogging where you jog for a while, and then walk for a while. After this you can work up to short runs, but don't push yourself too much in the beginning because, although you may not feel tired, you could be putting your body under strain. It's not advisable for anyone who

is under eighteen to attempt long-distance or marathon running because of the stress that this puts on the bones.

Whether you're racing or not, running can be very exhilarating, as long as you don't overstep yourself and try to run too far too soon!

RUNNERS' RULES

1. Always warm up before you run.
2. Run with a companion – you should be able to carry on a conversation as you jog along. If you can't, you're pushing too hard.
3. Don't run after a heavy meal or if you're feeling very weak and tired.
4. Try to avoid running too far on hard pavements – try the park or grass verges instead.

What to Wear

To make running safe you must make sure you have a pair of training shoes that were built for the job with firm, thickly cushioned soles. Wear comfortable clothes, and if it is cold remember that several layers are warmer than one thick layer. You can always take a tracksuit top off and tie it around your waist when things hot up. If possible it's best to wear cotton next to the skin since this absorbs perspiration and keeps you feeling cool and comfortable.

RAMBLING ON

Walking is one of the most underrated activities when it comes to fitness; a pity when we can all do it from an early age without any training at all! Rambling is a sport that can be enjoyed by all ages. Walking in the countryside gives you the benefits of fresh air, interesting scenery and good exercise. Of course going off on a long distance ramble is not something you take as lightly as a trek around the local park. It needs planning, and a willing adult to act as guide. Rambling is something you might want to suggest to your parents or teachers because it is a group activity (never something to do alone).

Before you go off on a long walk you will have to plan your route. Your group leader will choose the route bearing in mind the availability of paths or open country. It isn't wise to walk long distances on roads – the surface is always hard on the feet, and it isn't easy to relax and enjoy the view when you have to worry about traffic. When you're plotting your route and working out how long it will take it's worth adding extra time for muddy terrain, stiles or bad weather! Remember that it's essential for the group to stick together, so you can only go as fast as the slowest member of the group.

As far as clothing goes, training shoes and a light waterproof jacket over your usual clothes should be enough for short country walks. If you plan to do a lot of walking, though, you may want to invest in strong walking shoes. Other than that all you need is a good map, a compass, a back-pack for food etcetera, and you're all set to step out!

27

BALLET

& DANCE

You only have to watch ballet dancers leaping energetically across a stage to realise that ballet can be an enjoyable and invigorating form of exercise. What isn't immediately apparent is the fact that a lot of less spectacular, but very important (and sometimes pretty gruelling), training goes on at the barre behind the scenes. A lot of the movements of ballet are used in keep-fit sessions nowadays, because ballet is a good way of getting supple and staying fit. In fact ballet tones up all the muscles of the body.

As with any exercise, when you take up ballet you shouldn't try to push yourself too hard (although you will need regular practice sessions if you really want to take it seriously). Many girls rush to get on to dancing 'on points', but this takes years of training and getting the muscles in shape. Your teacher will advise you, and tell you that the development of the muscles of your foot, the structure of the foot itself, and the length of your toes must be taken into consideration before you can dance on points. It definitely isn't something you should ever try to do at home.

Ballet is excellent training for sports, though it might not seem it at first glance! If you practise ballet movements regularly the thighs will become stronger and sports that depend on leg strength like running, tennis and skating will seem much easier. Ballet is also a great way of improving your posture, and helping you move better. It can also give you self-confidence and poise – what's more, if you love music, and sometimes feel like jumping for joy, ballet is a lot of fun!

THOROUGHLY MODERN MOVEMENT

If you would like to be able to move like the dancers on television programmes, and give your body a good 'workout' at the same time, you might want to consider modern dance, or jazz dance which is a progression of modern dance (both of these are sometimes called aerobic dancing). Modern dance is a combination of exercise and dance movements to develop a fit body and good stance – it's a great way to shake off your troubles and enjoy yourself too. Just as with ballet, you should be sure you have a

Left: *ballet school rehearsals.* Centre: *contemporary dance with the Royal Ballet School performing* The White Goddess. *Above: Sadler's Wells Royal Ballet dancing to ragtime music in* Elite Syncopations

qualified teacher, and you shouldn't be in too much of a rush to get on to the fancy acrobatic stuff you see on television before you've done the groundwork and are sure your muscles are strong enough.

The outfit you wear should be similar to that worn for ballet classes – you can buy special jazz dance shoes, but a soft ballet shoe will do just as well. Trainers usually won't do because they aren't flexible enough to allow you to use all the foot muscles when you're dancing. Bare feet may be all right, depending on the flooring – you should check this out with your dance teacher.

TU-TU MUCH ~ OR WHAT TO WEAR AT THE BARRE!

These days the training outfits for ballet are much the same as for keep-fit or modern dance. Stretchy leotards, tights and occasionally leg-warmers are worn. Tutus are only worn for exams and concerts. The one thing you must be sure about is that your shoes are a good fit – although ballet shoes must fit snugly they mustn't cramp your toes. When your feet are growing, ballet shoes need to be changed as often as your ordinary shoes. Generally it's best to buy the leather kind, or the cheaper canvas type for practising – the pretty satin shoes wear out too quickly and aren't practical for training.

Super girls need super-fuel! Just as an engine needs the right kind of fuel to keep ticking over at peak performance, so our bodies need the right kind of food if we want to be super-fit and energy-packed. So what makes up the right kind of fuel for busy bodies? The answer is food that is packed with body building goodies such as vitamins, minerals, protein and unrefined carbohydrates.

What's a Vitamin?

Vitamins are substances, present in food in its natural state in varying amounts, which are essential to our health and the proper working of all our body 'machinery'. If you eat a balanced diet, containing lots of fresh fruit, vegetables, wholemeal bread, whole cereals, lean meat, dairy foods and fish, you should get all the vital vitamins you need for energy and good health. Vitamin pills aren't usually necessary unless you have a special illness, or if you aren't eating as well as you should. Your doctor may advise vitamin pills at certain times, but generally your best bet is to eat lots of vitamin-packed food.

EAT UP

GOOD HEALTH ~
The ABC of vitamins

There are five main vitamins – vitamins A, C, D, E and the B team! All of them are important if you want to feel super-fit.

★ **Vitamin A** is often called the 'growth vitamin' because it is essential for healthy growth and also for healthy skin, gums and eyes. You'll find it in milk, butter, margarine, carrots, fish and spinach among other foods.

★ **The B team** is a group of vitamins which act together to help in the growing process and help to look after the skin, hair, digestion, and many bodily processes. You'll find the busy B vitamins in liver, kidney, wheatgerm, wholemeal bread and brewer's yeast. You need to eat some food containing all the B vitamins every day because they are water-soluble vitamins, which means your body flushes them out each day, and constantly requires fresh supplies.

★ **Vitamin C** is the best known vitamin. It is said to help fight infections and many people believe it helps to prevent colds, though doctors aren't convinced about that one. It is needed for the health of all our body cells because it helps our skin to mend and renew itself, protects gums and teeth and helps keep up energy levels. Like the B vitamins, vitamin C is water-soluble, so you need to eat some vitamin-C rich food each day. The best sources are oranges, lemons and grapefruit, and fresh green vegetables like cabbage and brussel sprouts. Potatoes also contain vitamin C.

★ **Vitamin D** is the vitamin that's vital for healthy bones and teeth. It's also said to help wounds to heal. You can find vitamin D in eggs, butter, margarine, milk and fish oils. Sunlight also helps our bodies to produce vitamin D.

★ **Vitamin E** is a vitamin that some health experts claim is a miracle worker. Its uses are not completely understood yet, but it is said to protect our body cells from damage. It's thought to be useful for improving energy levels. Good sources of vitamin E are wheatgerm, wholemeal bread, leafy green vegetables and egg yolk.

Health down the drain

Unfortunately we don't always get all the goodness we ought to get from our food because vitamins can easily be destroyed. When you cook vegetables some of the vitamin C is destroyed by heating, and much of it escapes into the cooking water. So rather than throw this down the drain, let it cool and drink it. It's a good idea to eat the skin of fruits too, since the vitamins often lie just under the skins, so if you peel too much off you'll miss out. This doesn't apply to oranges and bananas, of course!

It's also a good idea to spare the knife if you're making a salad, and just break open lettuces with your fingers, since even the touch of cold steel can cause a loss of vitamin C. Do try to eat your food as soon as possible (without gobbling!) after it's been prepared because food left standing around can lose vitamins too.

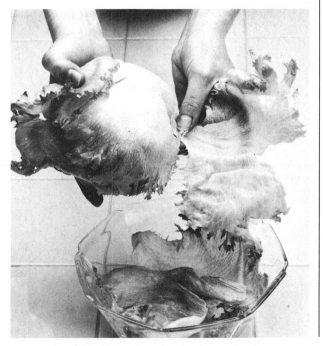

MINERALS
~who needs them?

The answer to that one is, we all do! While most folk know that we need to get vitamins from our food, many people still aren't aware of the fact that minerals like iron, calcium and zinc are just as important for our well-being. Minerals are substances needed for many body functions but which can't be made by our bodies. We depend on getting vital minerals from our food and water. We can get calcium, which we need for healthy teeth and bones, from milk, milk products, nuts and sesame seeds. Iron, which is needed particularly by girls who have started their periods, can be found in liver, kidneys, meat, wheatgerm, shellfish and watercress. Zinc, which is needed for those who are growing fast, is found in meat, fish, lentils, green leafy vegetables, wheatgerm, nuts, seeds and cheddar cheese.

PROTEIN
~power plus!

Our bodies are made up of about 20% protein and when you are still growing you need to make sure you're eating enough protein-rich body-building food. You need protein to look good and feel good – it makes up our skin, hair, nails, muscles and maintains many of the body's functions.

High power protein foods for you to eat are eggs, milk, meat, fish, whole grains, soya products, seeds, peas, beans and lentils. It's a good idea to make sure you get some form of protein food at every meal – especially breakfast (an important meal for super kids!). A good whole grain cereal (muesli or porridge, perhaps) will give you the energy you need to face up to busy mornings (yes, even Monday mornings) and will help prevent that tired 'brain-fagged' feeling before lunchtime.

POW
~it's a carbohydrate

Carbohydrates – contained in starchy foods like bread, potatoes and cereals – are essential if you want to feel bursting with energy. But it's a fact that you can get too much of a good thing, and too many starchy foods leave you fat, not fit! To be sure you're getting the right sort of carbohydrates go for the high-fibre starchy foods like wholemeal bread, potatoes in their jackets, whole grain rice and pasta, and avoid the stodgy, useless, podge-making carbohydrates like biscuits and cakes.

Green leafy vegetables are packed with energy-giving vitamins and minerals. So eat lots of the green stuff!

KER-RUNCH!
~fibre fitness

Crunchy, natural, unrefined food is the best for you – and one reason for this is because whole foods contain more fibre. Fibre is a mixture of plant substances – you could say it is like the skeleton of a plant because it holds the plant upright! Fibre is important to us in that it prevents various digestive and other troubles, and, as Granny might put it, 'keeps us regular'. It is also said to help those who want to keep their weight down without going hungry because it makes you feel fuller, *and* takes longer to eat. To test this for yourself, chew a slice of low-fibre white bread, then a slice of wholemeal bread, which is high in fibre. You can make the brown bread last much longer, and, when it comes to the crunch it is much more tasty and satisfying. For fitness inside and out make sure you get a high-fibre diet by being chew-sy about what you eat and include lots of crunchy vegetables, wholemeal bread, and nuts in your meals.

SWEET NOTHINGS

Sweet foods may be tempting, but the plain fact is, they're the foods to cut down on if you want to be super-fit and energy-packed. People used to believe that a spoonful of sugar not only helped the medicine go down, but also gave extra energy. It's now known that this isn't so – while eating something sweet might give you a swift boost of energy, it will later rob you of energy, and give you that 'flagging' feeling. Sweet foods are energy-drainers in the long run. Not only that, sugary food is known to be dangerous for the teeth. If you have a sweet tooth, and want to stay lively and keep smiling, it's best to eat sweet fruits like apples and bananas when you fancy a sweet treat.

ZAPPY SNACKS

There comes a moment when most of us feel like a nibble between meals to keep energy levels up. If you want an energy-boosting snack after school and before a sports session or a dance lesson, for instance, it isn't wise to head for the sweet shop. Melt-in-the-mouth crisps and sweets aren't that satisfying when you think about it! It's much better to go for a sustaining snack that will give you the power boost you need when you need it. Light snacks to try include nuts and raisins, bags of dried fruit and sunflower seeds, sesame seed bars, slices of cheese, bananas, apples, oranges or pot of yogurt. Pack something like this in your lunch box instead of chocolate bars and biscuits and you'll soon feel, and look, more super-charged!

GOOD OLD JACK SPRAT ...

. . . was thinking on the right lines when he turned up his nose at fatty foods. Health experts agree that on average we eat far too much fat for our own good. Fat contains twice the number of calories per ounce than any other food and it is thought that eating too much saturated fat found in meat and dairy produce may cause heart disease. For those who want to be super-fit, it's essential to start cutting down on fatty foods as soon as possible. Don't eat chips, crisps, chocolate and 'fry-up' meals every day. You can get all the fat you need from moderate amounts of butter, margarine, oily fish, beans, nuts and cheese.

Recipes for HEALTH

Sprouting out!

Sprouted beans and seeds are vitamin and mineral-packed and extremely low in calories. The bean or seed sprouts contain lots of valuable nutrients to feed the growing plant – and these nutrients are just as useful for growing kids!

You can buy beans and seeds for sprouting from health food shops – the most common ones used are alfalfa seeds, chick peas, lentils, mung and aduki beans.

To sprout the beans or seeds simply put them in a clean jam jar (to be sure they have enough space to grow put only about a tablespoonful in the jar). Fill the jar with water, then place a piece of muslin over the top of the jam jar and secure with an elastic band. Soak them overnight, then turn the jam jar upside down to drain it, and keep the jar in a dark place that's neither too hot or too cold (a kitchen cupboard will do). Simply rinse them three times a day and they should be ready to eat after about five days. Try them in salads, in toasted cheese sandwiches – they're great with crunchy peanut butter too!

Cheese Balls

These fruity cheese balls in crunchy sesame seeds are packed with calcium, and taste like mini cheesecakes. They're a great teatime snack. To make about 8–10 balls you'll need:

2oz (50g) raisins
1 tablespoon of wheat bran
1 lemon or 1 small orange
pinch of mixed spice
4oz (100g) low-fat soft cheese
1oz (25g) of sesame seeds

Chop the raisins finely and mix them with the wheat bran. Wash the orange or lemon well, then grate the rind into the dried fruit mixture. Add the pinch of spice and blend in the cheese. Use your hands to roll the mixture into balls and then roll them in the sesame seeds. Chill them in the fridge before eating.

Energy Milkshake

Drink to your health with this high-powered shake. You'll need:

1 banana
juice of half an orange
2 tablespoons pineapple juice
½ pint (300ml) of milk
chopped nuts (optional)

Mash the banana and add the orange juice, pineapple juice and then the milk. Whisk up well and pour into a tall glass, top off with a few chopped or flaked nuts, if required.

Food for sport

All professional athletes know the value of a good balanced diet with lots of fresh fruit and vegetables for vitality, protein for muscle building and carbohydrates like bread and pasta to provide the energy you need for extra muscle power when it counts. Food has always played an important part in sport – rugby players traditionally eat oranges at half-time, footballers down pints of milk, and marathon runners often eat pasta the day before a big race to improve their staying power. No-one has proved that eating specific foods actually makes you better at sport, but if you want to excel in some sport it's a good idea to strengthen your body, and make sure you're eating wisely and well.

YOUR EXTRA ENERGY EATING PLAN!

●●●●●●●●●●●●●● PLAN! ●●●●●●●●●●●●●●

Breakfast – porridge with milk, a teaspoon of honey and fresh fruit, *or* egg, wholemeal toast, fruit juice, *or* muesli with chopped banana, milk, wholemeal toast and honey or a savoury spread.

Elevenses' treat – milk plus a choice of: apple, orange, banana, natural muesli bar, bag of nuts and raisins.

Lunch – meat, fish, cheese or vegetable pie, with two vegetables, or mixed salad (avoid

Here's a suggestion for a day's high-vitality eating . . .

chips), *or* stuffed jacket potato, *or* packed lunch with wholemeal sandwiches (with meat, egg, fish or cheese filling) salad, fruit and yogurt.

4 o'clock filler – choose from apple, orange, nuts and raisins, sesame seed bar, slice wholemeal bread and honey or savoury spread.

Supper – any protein food (meat, fish, beans, lentils, cheese, chicken etc) or wholemeal quiche with two lightly-cooked vegetables, wholemeal pasta with sauce, stuffed vegetables, wholemeal pizza or a casserole. Cheesecake, crumble, fresh or stewed fruit, mousse or yoghurt.

Drinks throughout the day: drink lots of water, fruit juice, milk or pep-u-up herb teas like rosehip or peppermint, sweetened with honey.

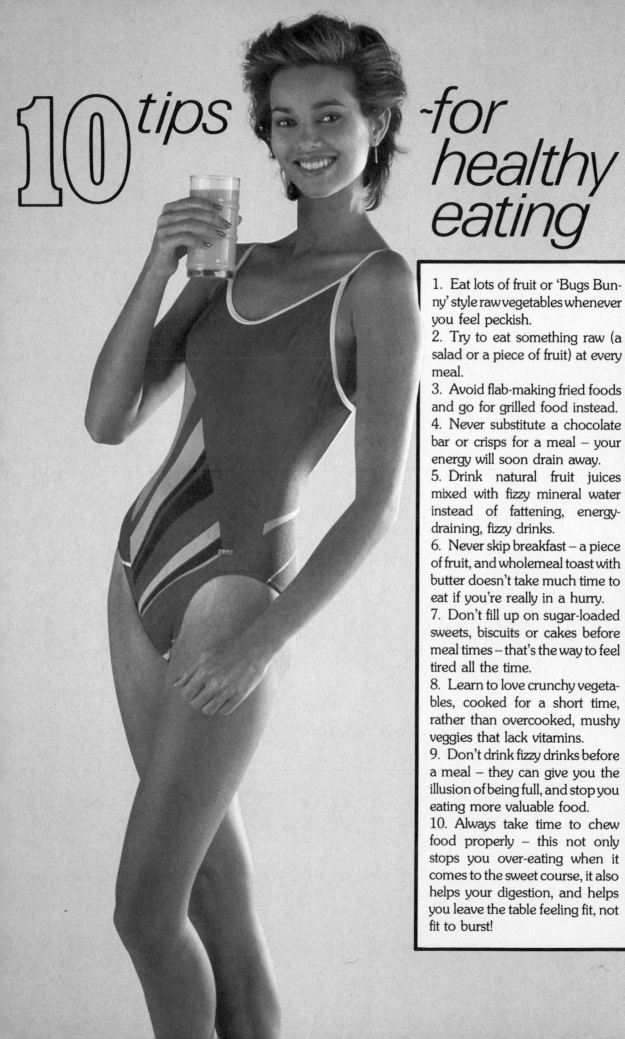

10 tips for healthy eating

1. Eat lots of fruit or 'Bugs Bunny' style raw vegetables whenever you feel peckish.

2. Try to eat something raw (a salad or a piece of fruit) at every meal.

3. Avoid flab-making fried foods and go for grilled food instead.

4. Never substitute a chocolate bar or crisps for a meal – your energy will soon drain away.

5. Drink natural fruit juices mixed with fizzy mineral water instead of fattening, energy-draining, fizzy drinks.

6. Never skip breakfast – a piece of fruit, and wholemeal toast with butter doesn't take much time to eat if you're really in a hurry.

7. Don't fill up on sugar-loaded sweets, biscuits or cakes before meal times – that's the way to feel tired all the time.

8. Learn to love crunchy vegetables, cooked for a short time, rather than overcooked, mushy veggies that lack vitamins.

9. Don't drink fizzy drinks before a meal – they can give you the illusion of being full, and stop you eating more valuable food.

10. Always take time to chew food properly – this not only stops you over-eating when it comes to the sweet course, it also helps your digestion, and helps you leave the table feeling fit, not fit to burst!

LOOKING GOOD...
FEELING GREAT

We've all heard that old phrase 'glowing with health', and it's a description we'd all like to live up to! Good health shows in your skin, hair, *eyes* – in short, you can't look good if you feel bad. If you're already eating sensibly, and taking some exercise, you're well on the way to having glossy hair, a good figure, and glowing skin. In this section we're going to look at ways you can give your looks extra polish, and give yourself that *extra* touch of get-up-and-glow using simple, home-made beauty treatments.

Skin deep

Your skin reflects the way you feel, and your general health. That means that anything that's good for you is good for your skin too – from outdoor exercise to a healthy balanced diet containing lots of fruit and vegetables. Foods that are particularly good for the skin are those rich in vitamins – vitamins A, B, and C particularly – so eat fruit and vegetables containing these vitamins for the sake of your skin.

Save Your Skin

Your skin does sometimes need a little extra protection against wind 'n' weather if you're the sporty, outdoor type. Use an all-purpose moisturising cream on your face when you're out in windy or chilly weather, and use a sunscreen product when exercising in the fresh air in Summer. That way your exercise sessions will leave you with a smooth skin as well as a sleek shape.

Spot On

Spots are the scourge of many a young skin but they can be avoided if you take extra care of your complexion. Our skins tend to get spottier when our bodies are going through the changes that take us from childhood to adulthood. To understand the reason why, it helps to take a look at how our skin is made up . . .

Skin consists of two main layers, and the top layer, or epidermis, is made up of cells that are constantly being renewed – the old dead cells are whisked away each time we wash. In the lower layer of skin, called the dermis, there are oil glands, nerves, sweat glands, blood vessels and hair follicles. Spots and blackheads start when the pores, or the openings of the hair follicles, are blocked by oil. This can happen when the oil glands are pouring out a lot of oil, as they tend to do around puberty. Also about this time in our lives the top layer of skin tends to speed up its shedding and renewing of cells and the dead cells on the surface can combine with oil to block the pores and build up lumps, bumps and pimples. If none of that sounds too pretty, remember that by keeping the pore openings clean you can do a lot to stop these trouble-making blockages and get away spot-free!

No skin can look its best if it isn't really clean. That might sound like a pretty obvious statement, but it's amazing how many folk don't bother to cleanse their skin properly. A swift once-over with the flannel won't do if you want your skin to have that extra glow. Ideally you should use an unperfumed soap or special cleanser for the face. Highly perfumed toilet soaps may smell nice but they can cause irritation on some skins; it's something to consider if you get odd rashes, blotches and dry patches. Always rinse your face well after cleansing – thirty splashes in warm water is best. Then dry carefully, patting with a clean towel.

Mask-A-Raid!

If your skin is dull and you tend to get blackheads and other lumps and bumps, you might want to try raiding the larder, and deep-cleansing your skin with a home-made face-pack. These can help unblock pores, and make your skin look a little more in the pink. You can make a simple, but effective face-pack from common things found in the kitchen – egg white, honey, or yogurt for instance, smoothed on the face then rinsed off after ten minutes, are good deep cleansers, and as effective at perking up your skin as anything you can buy.

You Need a Good Scrub!

A facial scrub helps your skin look fresher by getting rid of the dull skin cells that might block pores. The easiest ever facial scrub is oatmeal – just add about a dessert spoonful to the lather when you're washing your face with your usual soap. Pay particular attention to the chin, and around the nose, where blackheads hide.

Come Clean

1

2

3

1. *For a deep cleansing facial sauna, add fresh mint or lavender to a bowl of boiling water.*

2. *Cover your head and the bowl with a towel so none of the steam is lost. After five minutes pat your skin dry.*

40

The skin on your body deserves as much attention as that on your face. Remember that you'll need to cleanse the skin of stale perspiration after exercise – particularly if you suffer from a spotty back. Lather up after every exercise session where possible, and use a back brush or loofah to reach your back if your skin problems are all behind you!

Dingy-looking skin on elbows, heels and pen-pushers' fingers can be lightened and brightened with lemon juice. Just dip a flannel or cotton ball into pure lemon juice and rub away at problem areas.

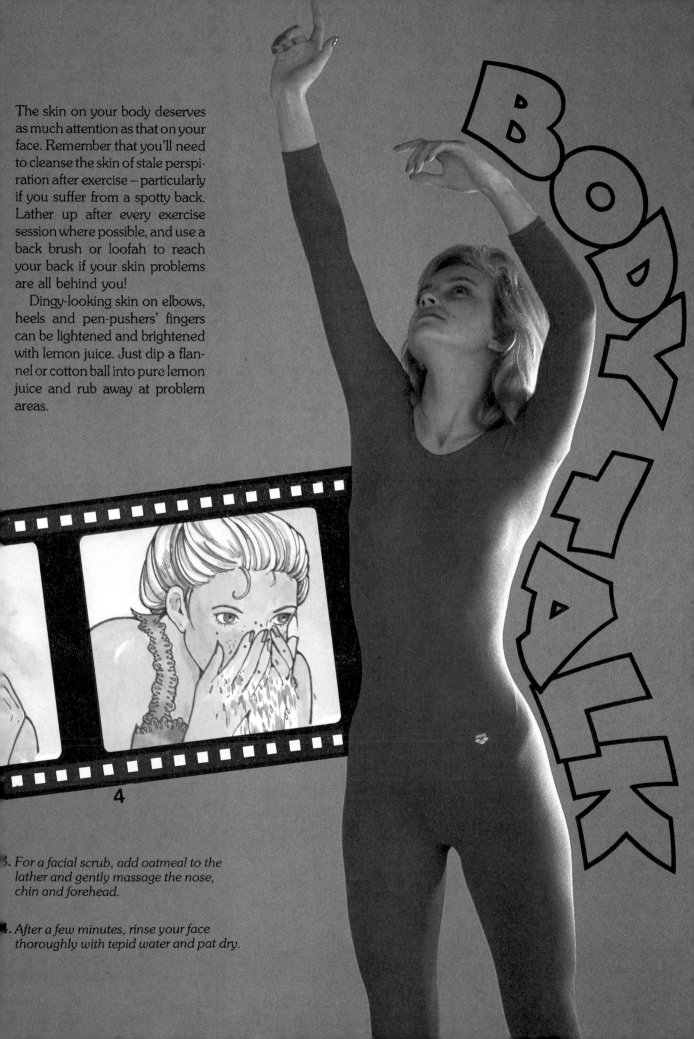

BODY TALK

4

3. *For a facial scrub, add oatmeal to the lather and gently massage the nose, chin and forehead.*

4. *After a few minutes, rinse your face thoroughly with tepid water and pat dry.*

The Way to Healthy Hair . . .
Whatever style you're going to choose, you've got to make sure that your hair has that extra sheen that comes from good health. Your hair, like your skin, reflects the state of your health – if you're bubbling over with energy, your hair is likely to be looking pretty bouncy too. Your hair is 'fed' at the roots by nutrients from your food. Exercise actually helps your hair because it gets the circulation ticking over nicely, which means a good supply of nutrients get through to your hair. These days many hairdressers don't just prescribe a good conditioner when hair is out of sorts, they advise on the right diet and exercise too. Some say standing on the head or hands does wonders to improve the look of the hair.

HAIR AND NOW

The good news for sporty super girls is that exercise can even help your hair look glossier and healthier. The bad news is that it can also make it look a fine mess unless you choose the right style to suit your busy and sporty life! Over the next few pages we're going to look at ways you can make sure your hair will stand up to sports (anything from a hectic dance session to a jog in the rain) and still come out shining!

Back to Basics
When you're brushing and combing your hair several times a day, it is worth making sure you've got the proper tools for the job. Often old, inexpensive hairbrushes with rough-edged, splitting nylon bristles will scratch at the hair and cause breakages. It's best, if possible, to get a natural bristle hairbrush, or a brush with plastic bristles with rounded ends. Choose a comb that doesn't have too much 'bite' – large combs with rounded, wide-spaced teeth are the best for your hair. Remember always to use a wide-toothed comb rather than a hairbrush to get through damp hair. Wet hair is more easily damaged because it is more stretchy, and so is easily broken. Don't pull with your comb at tangles, ease knots out with your fingers.

GO FOR GLOSS!

Finger and scrunch drying is less damaging to hair than using a hair dryer.

To stay looking shiny through wind, weather and rough treatment on the sports field, hair has to have the right protection, in the form of a good conditioner. It also needs to be thoroughly cleansed after particularly hectic exercise. Give your hair a shampoo every time you've been a little hot-headed and perspired a lot when exercising. Always make sure you shampoo your hair after a swim too – the chlorine in pool water and the salt in sea water can be drying on the hair and leave it looking dull.

If you can't always shampoo, at least give your hair a rinse in clear water after a swim (pack a plastic bottle of tap water for the purpose if there isn't a shower available).

If you're washing your hair quite often go for a gentle shampoo – there are lots on the market that only need to be lathered up once, and are designed to be used often (even every day). Always follow up your shampoo with a conditioning rinse if your hair is looking dry and dull thanks to too much sun and wind. If you hair is oily, and quickly looks lank and dull, you've got to be extra careful about washing your hair as often as possible – frequent shampooing won't make it more oily so long as you choose a gentle shampoo and a light, oil-free conditioner and rinse well.

Honey Hair Conditioner

You can make a good conditioner for dull hair by mixing 3 tablespoons of clear honey with 1 tablespoon of olive oil (or other vegetable oil). Mix thoroughly and massage into newly washed hair. Wrap the head in a warmed towel, leave for 15 minutes, and then rinse well.

Always towel dry your hair well (no vigorous rubbing, though, as you could cause tangling) before you use a blow-drier. Don't get the drier too near your hair – the heat can damage dry hair. If you like a sleek, straight style, make sure you direct the jet of air down the hair shaft – this helps to prevent those messy 'flyaway' ends. If you like a sporty, fluffy style it helps if you part-dry the

The way you dry your hair can make a lot of difference to the final look of your style.

hair with the head down, so that the air from your drier gives 'lift' to the underneath layers of your hair. Then, when the hair is almost dry, straighten up and blow dry, using an air-vented radial brush to shape the hair. Never concentrate the stream of air on one particular area – always move it around to prevent damaging your hair, and that hot-headed feeling!

GET SET

Most styles these days need that extra bit of help if they're to stay put through vigorous exercise routines or even disco-dancing. Luckily there are now lots of gells, mousses and hairsprays on the market designed to give your hairstyle extra staying power. Gels give a touch of extra hold to sleeked-back styles – good for tucking stragglers into a plait, for instance, or for making sure a spiky fringe doesn't flop into your eyes while you're dancing or rushing around the sports field.

Mousses can also give your hair extra firmness and body – although they usually give a less stiff effect than a gel. Mousses are good for reviving permed hair and for giving extra lift to 'high hair' layered styles when they're falling a bit flat.

Hairspray may sound a little old-fashioned, but it's coming into its own again. There are now hairsprays to give your hair a really firm hold and to help protect your style from the ravages of damp weather, humid discos, chilly ice rinks or steamed-up exercise classes!

JUST YOUR STYLE

If you want to be a good-looking sport you've got to choose your hairstyle with care. Hairstyles that need a lot of fuss are out if you want to run around a sports field, and bend 'n' stretch your way through an exercise session and still have your hair bounce back into shape. If you want to look neat while you get in shape, your hair's got to shape up too!

The Short Cut
Those ever-fashionable layered short cuts are really the easiest styles to manage for sporty types. They can help you feel cool-headed when things hot up since they have a little 'lift' on top, and air can circulate among the layers. Many professional skaters go for this type of off-the-face short style since it won't flop in cool atmospheres and won't get into their eyes. Likewise short styles are good for swimmers and those who take part in athletics. A layered style like the one in our picture is easy to manage and can be quickly blow-dried after exercising.

TAKE A LONG LOOK

If you like long hair, it's generally best to tie it back, or sweep it up and away from the face when you're exercising. Here are a couple of ways of keeping long-hair neat.

The Super Plait
1. Pull hair back and grip in place above and behind the ears. Divide topmost layer of hair into 3, and start to plait.

2. Continue to plait down the length gradually adding in the remaining hair as you plait.

The Ooh-la-la Pleat
1. Sweep all hair to one side.

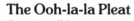

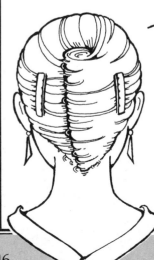

2. Fold it back towards the other side, and roll the hair into a long sausage shape. Secure with grips and hair spray.

IN THE MIDDLE

Mid-length hair can often be the most difficult to deal with when it comes to keeping it tidy during sports or exercise sessions. But even if your hair is not quite long enough to put on top, these two twirly styles will help keep it in place and looking pretty.

The Twister

1. Part hair in centre. Gather the hair into bunches with your hands (1 side at a time) and twirl tightly.

2. When the hair starts to turn back on itself, to form a little 'knot' at the end, secure with a grip or clamp.

The Wrap

1. Roughly divide the hair into 2 at the back. Take hold of a large section of hair at the temple and twirl it tightly.

2. Pull the twirled section around the back and gradually add in hair from underneath as you twirl. Wrap the back hair over it, and secure with grips. Repeat on other side, and hide the join by folding over a strand of hair from the nape.

GRIPPING STUFF

You might not fancy the idea of a clip around the ear or a firm grip on your hair, but the fact is hair grips, clips and clamps are useful for sporty types who want to keep their style in place. Go for hair grips with cushioned ends – you can find them to match your hair colour, or you can get brightly coloured ones if you prefer to show them off.

Decorative clamps are the fashionable way of tidying hair from the face when you're dancing – the 'crocodile' teeth give a strong grip. Combs too are useful for tidying stray 'wisps' – add a little mousse to the hair to give combs extra staying power. If you simply want to tie your hair back, go for fabric covered elastic ponytail bands – much kinder to your hair than ordinary elastic bands.

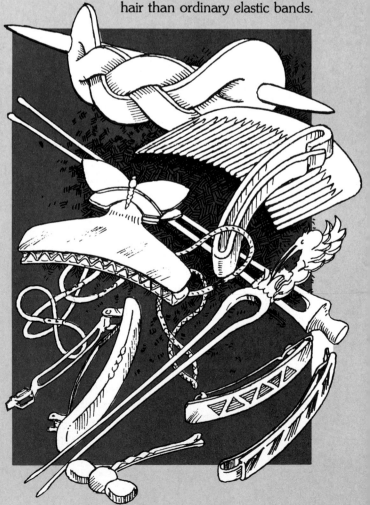

Not many of us are happy with the way our figure shapes up, and the most common complaint is that there's too much flab! Luckily, if you exercise and are careful about what you eat, you can soon have a neat figure and shape up nicely.

Puppy-fat . . . Fat Chance!

If you're a little more plump than you'd like to be, it's an idea to check that you really are eating sensibly and exercising enough. It would be nice to be able to put your weighty problems down to 'puppy-fat' and to say that you'll grow out of your plumpness. Unfortunately though, doctors these days say that young people usually don't grow out of being overweight unless they resolve to do something about their excess poundage. Plumpness is not usually anything to do with 'trouble with the glands' as you grow up. Some people simply inherit the ability to put on weight more easily – while others

FIGURE IT OUT

48

seem to be able to eat and eat and never gain too much weight.

If you are one of the unlucky folk who seem to gain weight at the sight of a cream cake, it is worth working out how you can improve your diet without feeling hungry, or depriving yourself of the important foods you need for vitality. The best way of doing this is to cut down on high-calorie 'junk' foods, and fill up on satisfying high-fibre foods like fruit and vegetables which have a lot of bulk for fewer calories.

What's a Calorie then?
A calorie is a unit used for measuring the amount of energy in our food. And here we aren't talking about vitality, but about the basic energy which the body needs to fuel all its various functions. These days another way of measuring the energy in food is by kilojoules – there are approximately 4.2 kilojoules to a calorie.

We all need a certain number of calories each day to keep our bodies moving and working properly, and to keep us feeling fit. However, if we take in more calories than we need, the surplus energy is stored on our bodies as fat.

The amount of calories needed varies from one person to another. If you're a very athletic type, always on the move, you'll obviously need more calories than folk who're less active.

How to Beat the Bulges . . .
If you feel you're too plump the first thing to do is to use up some of the stored energy that your intake of calories has given you, by taking more regular exercise.

It's also a good idea to eat less of the calorie-loaded foods, and more of the highly nutritious vitality-packed foods (see Eat Up section). The one thing growing girls and boys should *never* do is try a drastic weight-reducing diet *or* skip meals in an effort to lose weight. Energy levels and your general health will suffer and, what's more, experts say over-strict slimming regimes just don't keep you slim in the long term!

If you are eating sensibly, and not bingeing on chocolate bars, and you are getting plenty of exercise, but you are still very overweight, it is always worth having a word with your doctor. But whatever you do don't go on a strict diet without medical help. Superkids should never go hungry!

How to cut calories

1. Substitute sweet fruits for sweets.
2. Start your meals with something raw and high in fibre – raw carrot, melon, salad or grapefruit are good starters to help you avoid second-helpings come the sweet course.
3. Avoid all the greasies – chips, crisps, fry-ups. Or if you do have fried food on occasion, drain it on kitchen paper to remove some oil first.
4. Drink fruit juice and mineral water instead of squash and sweetened fruit drinks.
5. Use a low-fat spread instead of margarine or butter and spread it thinly.
6. Try an extra glass of water at mealtimes to help you feel fuller.
7. Remember that things like ketchup, sauces and salad creams contain sugar and can add quite a few calories to your meals. Learn to love your food without the sauce!
8. Don't rush your meals – it takes about 20 minutes for your stomach to give your brain the message that its full!
9. Don't read or watch television while you eat – when you're distracted it's too easy to eat too quickly and over-eat.
10. Try eating natural yogurt or fresh fruit instead of puddings or cakes for afters.

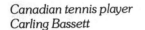
Canadian tennis player
Carling Bassett

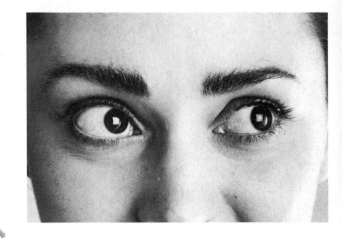

EYES RIGHT...

Good eyesight is important to everyone, but it's especially vital if you want to be good at sports. Regular eye tests are important. You probably have tests every so often at school, but if you feel your eyesight might not be as good as it could be – if, say, you're always screwing up your eyes to see the blackboard, or you sometimes can't see the ball coming your way in sports lessons – it's worth going along to an optician for a check-up. Even if your eyesight is good, it is always worth taking care to avoid eyestrain as this can give you headaches.

All About Health

If you want to be a super girl you've got to take care of your health. Life's too exciting, after all, to have days when you're ill, tired, bed-bound and generally out of the running! If you want to be sure to have all the energy you need for a full life it pays to make sure your body is in tip-top working condition and fighting fit!

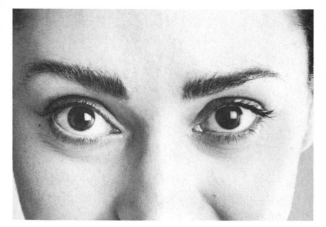

EYES BRIGHT...   ON SPECS...

To stay bright-eyed, and strain-free follow these three simple rules:

1. Always read or study in good lighting. You can't actually ruin your eyes by reading in the wrong light, but you can help your eyes to work better if you're careful about lighting. If you study at night always use a reading lamp, positioned behind one shoulder, so that it shines on to your books.

2. Take care when you're watching television. Too much television won't give you 'square eyes' or ruin your eyesight, but it can be a strain on the eyes. To avoid strain never watch in a completely darkened room – make sure there's at least one lamp shining. Don't watch television from the floor or sit too near the screen either. For your eyes' sake it's best to sit at least 5 feet away from the television, in a chair, so that you are sitting looking slightly down, rather than up, at the screen.

3. Don't wear fashion sunglasses for any length of time as they can distort your vision (this can be particularly dangerous crossing roads or when you're riding a bike). Avoid the glasses with coloured lenses and always go for grey or brown since these distort the vision least. Mostly you won't need to wear sunglasses, but if you find you are constantly complaining of the glare, and your eyes water when you're out in the sun, it would be worth going along to an optician to see if he or she prescribes special sunglasses to protect your eyes from the sun.

If you need spectacles, you needn't think that that's the end of your sporting career! Girls and boys who wear glasses can make passes, and score goals, if they wear the right kind of eye gear. For cycling, running and so on you can probably wear your ordinary spectacles but they should have plastic lenses which won't shatter and are lighter than glass. Specs must fit well so they aren't likely to slide off at a crucial moment. Nowadays you can even get special sports goggles fitted with your own lenses from your optician – there are types for swimming and even for racket-games.

If you're over ten and you want to go in for more vigorous sports or dancing you may want to ask your optician about contact lenses. These are lenses which are placed on the eye and they stay in place by floating on the tear film. You can only really consider contact lenses, though, when you're sure you can handle them and look after them properly.

ARE CARROTS GOOD FOR YOUR EYES?

Carrots contain lots of vitamin A which is the vitamin said to help promote good eyesight and to form the substance that enables our eyes to adjust to darkness. It's said that if you don't get enough vitamin A your eyes are more prone to infections and inflammation around the lids.

51

TEETH...stop the rot

A nice smile is everyone's greatest asset. A pity, then, that many of us are afraid to smile because of dingy teeth, or a mouthful of fillings! From about the age of six our permanent teeth start to come through and these teeth should stay with us for life, so they need daily care to avoid damage.

If we're going to avoid toothache, fillings or, worse, lost teeth, we have to understand how teeth come to be damaged in the first place. Tooth decay occurs when the enamel coating of our teeth is attacked by plaque. Plaque is the 'furry-feeling' substance that forms on our teeth. Plaque forms a sticky layer on the teeth, containing millions of bacteria, and these bacteria combine with the sugar in our food to form an acid that literally eats away at our teeth. The way to stop the rot is to take care to clean the plaque from your teeth, and to cut down on sugary foods.

A Better Bite

If you want to be kind to your teeth it pays to let them bite into the right kind of food. Calcium-rich foods like cheese and other milky foods help new teeth to grow stronger. Crunchy raw vegetables, like a stick of celery or raw carrot, are also good for your teeth.

They stimulate the gums and, since you have to chew them well, bring about an increase in saliva which dilutes the acids that attack your teeth.

It was once thought that eating apples was the natural way of cleaning the teeth, but dentists now say that biting into an apple doesn't get rid of plaque. (Eating sweet fruit is preferable to eating sweets though.) If you like to have something to chew occasionally it's best to avoid sugary chewing gums and to go instead for the sugar-free gums you now find in the shops. Again chewing gum of this kind is much better for your teeth than chewing sweets!

Get your teeth into crunchy vegetables and give them a treat!

KEEP SMILING

Follow these rules for healthy teeth:

1. Brush teeth with fluoride toothpaste at least twice a day.

2. Take extra care brushing teeth when they're 'wobbly' and permanent teeth are pushing through. This does *not* mean avoiding brushing wobbly teeth or sore gums. If you avoid 'wobbly' teeth plaque can run riot!

3. Save sweets for mealtimes only – don't nibble them between meals.

4. If you are tempted by a bag of sweets *don't* make them last throughout the day – eat them all at once so that there is only one acid attack on your teeth, not several.

5. Make sure you clean right up into the gums when brushing teeth or you may lose teeth through gum disease (if gums bleed it's a sign you need to clean them more thoroughly).

6. Floss your teeth to remove any food that's stuck. Ask your dentist to show you how.

7. Never scrub too hard at the teeth with a hard toothbrush – soft/medium bristles are best.

8. Change toothbrushes *every* 3 months.

9. Try coloured disclosing tablets to see where plaque lurks.

10. Visit your dentist *every* 6 months for a check-up.

BRUSH UP ON TEETH

Do you know how to clean your teeth? That may sound like a silly question but dentists tell us that many of us are simply not brushing our teeth properly and are leaving behind trouble-making plaque.

This is the way to brush your teeth if you want to beat the demon plaque!

1. Apply toothpaste to a *dry* brush, then, using short, gently back and forth movements, cleanse the outside surfaces of the upper and lower teeth – pay special attention to the places where teeth and gums meet, since plaque can lodge there.

2. Then cleanse the inside surface of all the upper teeth with the same short, gently back 'n' forth movement.

3. Next clean the inner surfaces of your lower teeth, tilting the brush.

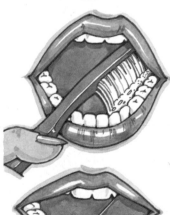

4. Finally brush the biting surfaces of upper and lower teeth with short, gently back and forth strokes.

Ideally you should brush your teeth for about 3 minutes – taking an egg-timer into the bathroom might help you do a more thorough job.

BEST FOOT

No would-be athlete or dancer should ever overlook their feet (and nor should super kids). The kind of shoes you wear when exercising or taking part in a sport are crucial if you want to avoid foot problems. Likewise the shoes you wear every day must be just right for you if you want to look after your feet.

First of all you must make sure you are wearing shoes that are big enough with plenty room for your toes to move. Pointed-toed shoes, for instance, may look nice, but they could lead to ugly and troublesome feet later on if you cram growing toes into them every day. You should always stand and walk in shoes when you're trying them on in the shop – shoes for everyday wear should be as wide as the widest part of your foot (by the first joint of the big toe) and should be at least $\frac{1}{2}$ inch (14 mm) longer than your foot to give your feet room to expand.

If you wear the right kind of shoes you can avoid

Exercise your feet

Here are four movements for feet to tone up weak muscles and strengthen the arches.
1. Rise up on tiptoes, with feet parallel, toes pointing straight ahead, then *slowly* lower.
2. Walk on the outsides of the feet to tone up the muscles. Try to walk about half way across your living room.
3. Stand on a thick book with your toes hanging over the edge. Bend the toes down as far as possible. Do this a couple of times.
4. Point one toe, then relax it slightly – then slowly rotate the foot from the ankle as if you're trying to draw a circle with your big toe. Move the foot one way, then the other. Change feet and start again.

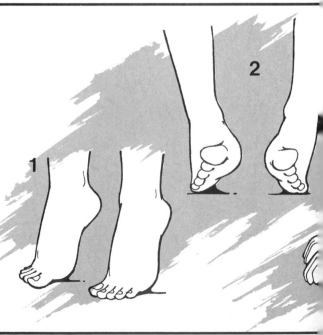

FORWARD

painful hard-skin conditions like corns and callouses. It's also a good idea to go barefoot sometimes too, to allow the feet to stretch themselves. Try to walk around the house without shoes or socks if the flooring allows. It's also a good idea to change your shoes quite often – especially if you wear shoes with heels. Swap over to flatties from time to time to give feet a little relief (it's also good for the shape of your legs if you vary the height of your heels).

CARING FOR FEET

Your poor down-trodden feet need as much care as the rest of your body. Here's how to look after them!

1. Wash your feet every day (and after exercising). Dry them well, especially between the toes, and then dust them with talcum powder.

2. Change socks or tights every day to keep feet feeling fresh.

3. Cut your toenails into a straight line. Don't cut fancy curves which might cut down too deep and cause trouble with the nails.

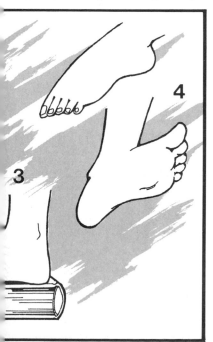

Ear, Ear...

Ears are important parts of the body for sporty types – not only are they the organs of hearing, but also of balance. Luckily we don't have to do a lot to keep our ears functioning properly. In fact, the less you do to your ears the better! You should, of course, wash the outer ear, but you should never try to clean right into the ear with the corner of towels, cotton buds and the like. The inner ear cleanses itself without our help.

If you go swimming a lot – every day for instance – it can be an idea to ask an expert at the pool about swimmers' ear plugs to prevent too much water in the ear. Alternatively you can used greased cotton wool. But if you only swim every so often, there is no need to worry if a little water gets into the ear – it will quickly drain away.

SLEEP TIGHT

When life's interesting, and there's lots to do, going to bed early might seem like a waste of time. But the fact is getting plenty of sleep is vital for our health and vitality. As we sleep the tissues and organs inside the body are busy growing and renewing themselves. The younger you are the more sleep you need to give your body a chance to grow and your organs a chance to rest and recharge. After a good night's sleep you will feel more lively and look it too.

Getting too little sleep results in that sluggish feeling when you don't really seem to be able to concentrate on anything. The occasional late night won't do much harm, since you can generally catch up on lost sleep over the next few nights. Making a habit of late nights, though, will mean your body and brain can never really operate at full power, so schoolwork, sports, and just about every part of your life will suffer. If you don't always feel bright-eyed and bouncing with health, it could be worth turning in early for a couple of nights to see what a little extra sleep can do for your health and appearance.

Need to Count Sheep?
We all have odd times when we can't get to sleep. Maybe you've been reading something exciting, or watching something scary . . . Or maybe you've got a problem, or something exciting coming up that's playing on your mind. The worst thing you can do when you can't sleep is to worry about it — getting all tensed up about not sleeping just means you're less likely to drop off. The thing to do is to switch your mind off, relax and just enjoy being in bed, able to lie there and do absolutely nothing for a change!

10 steps to a good night's sleep

1. Wind down before bedtime. Don't take any vigorous exercise within an hour or two of bedtime, although it's a good idea to exercise earlier in the day to help you sleep.

2. Don't watch horror films or read adventure stories at bedtime.

3. Have a warm milky drink and a light starchy snack (a wholemeal biscuit, perhaps) just before bedtime.

4. Don't eat a big fatty meal (fish 'n' chips for instance) within two hours of bedtime – your churning tum will keep you awake!

5. Keep warm in bed – bed socks or a hot water bottle are a good idea! But make sure the room isn't too stuffy. If the room is centrally-heated put a bowl of water by the radiator.

6. Have a warm bath before bedtime.

7. If you tend to toss and turn make sure you don't have too many bedclothes on the bed.

8. Surround yourself with all the things you like in your bedroom – from old 'Ted' to favourite posters. Make it your own relaxing retreat.

9. If you tend to worry and mull things over at bedtime, keep a note-pad by the bed to jot things down on. Jotting down odd thoughts sometimes helps you to relax and forget them.

10. Don't panic if you don't drop off right away, just flop and concentrate on feeling every part of your body slowly relax.

SLEEPY-TIME EXERCISES

Try these exercises next time you can't sleep:

1. The Big Flop – lie on your back in bed and tighten every muscle. Clench your fists, flex your arms, tighten the buttocks, point your toes, grit your teeth. Now, starting at the feet, slowly relax the muscles – let the feet fall to the sides naturally, feel the knees loosen etcetera. Work right up until you slacken your jaw. You can now be sure your body is in a really sleepy mood.

2. Lift the lid – open your eyes wide and stare at a spot on the ceiling for the count of 10. Then close your eyes. Open again and stare at the same spot for a count of 10. Repeat until the lids drop!

JUST A BREATH OF FRESH AIR

Parents and teachers are always telling you that getting out into the fresh air is good for you . . . But are they right? Well, you can test it for yourself. When you're feeling sluggish and bored, step out for a breath of fresh air – you'll probably find that it blows away the cobwebs and helps you feel much brighter. When you feel tired it is tempting to just sit around by the fire, or to lie about half the morning in bed, but this can actually make you feel more tired and lethargic.

The oxygen in the air you breathe helps to burn the food you eat and turn it into energy, and, through the bloodstream, it also helps carry nutrients to skin, hair and all your body's cells. Oxygen also refreshes the brain – so try a breath of air when you're feeling foggy and befuddled!

Everyone has the odd black mood now and then, but luckily there is a lot that you can do to make life seem a little rosier. Exercise, for one thing, can perk you up and give you the kind of tingle that makes you feel much more lively and optimistic. Many folk find they can literally run away from that down-in-the-dumps feeling!

When you're feeling extremely

MOODS
How to zap out of them

angry with someone exercise can help you work off those feelings too. Instead of letting these feelings build up or blowing your top and saying something you may regret, vigorous exercise like skipping or dancing should help you cool down!

It could be that your low mood is just due to tiredness, or tension, because of some important event coming up. It's worth trying to get a little extra sleep, and also learning to relax. If you're feeling really tense and anxious before an exam, or taking part in some competition, try consciously to decide to stop panicking. Try to clear your mind and take a couple of deep breaths, concentrating on nothing more than your stomach rising and falling. When you're 'worked up' you tend to breathe shallowly which makes the chest rise and fall, and sends 'panic stations' messages to your brain. Stop all this happening by breathing the way sleeping cats and dogs do – right from the stomach. You shouldn't feel your chest rise at all when you breathe, except after really vigorous exercise. Supergirls who want to stay cool in sticky situations should make sure their breath doesn't come in short pants!

TAKE A BREATHER

**Try the following deep-breathing exercise
any time you're all 'strung-up'!**

1. Sit up in a comfortable arm chair, or lie down with your head on a pillow in a quiet, warm room away from any draughts.

2. Breathe in deeply with one hand placed on your chest, and the other one on the upper part of your stomach. Concentrate on trying to push the air down into your 'stomach' and feel your diaphragm rise under your lower hand.

3. Breathe out gently, taking slightly longer over doing this than you did over breathing in. Purse your lips to let the last of the breath blow out. Feel your stomach drop back under your hand.

4. Wait a minute then breathe in and out gently once more – you should no longer feel tense.

This is an instant calmer for those moments when you're edgy and nervous. It's also good training for proper breathing. Practise the movement in odd moments and you'll soon learn how to breathe properly for your health's sake. Remember many sports, like swimming, aerobics and so on, rely on good breathing too.

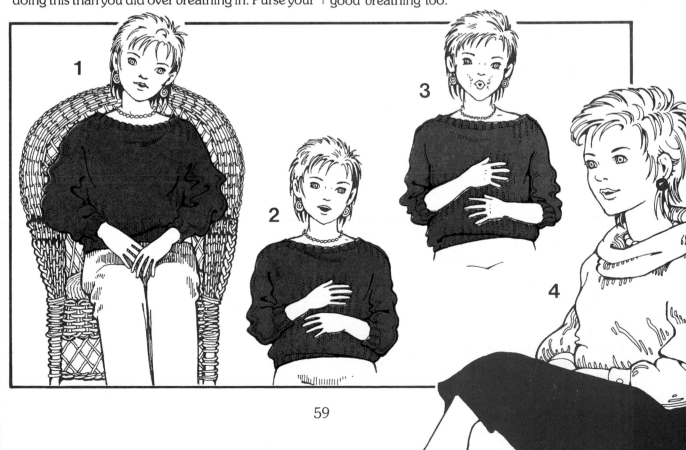

GROWING

Rightly or wrongly, most teenagers can't wait to grow up, so they tend to find the lengthy process of growing up a bit of a bore. It's like a long journey when you can't wait to get to your destination. Of course journeys themselves can be enjoyable – something you might overlook if you've simply set

UP – DOES IT HAVE TO BE A PAIN?

TOP 10 TIPS FOR SUPER GIRLS

If you want to look good, be fit and feel super-charged you've got to take good care of yourself. Make sure you follow these ten super tips!

1. Eat lots of natural, wholesome body-building foods like vegatables, fresh fruit, cereals, meat, fish, dairy products and eggs.

2. Avoid eating sugary foods that can sap your energy (and in the long run ruin your smile).

3. Be proud of your body, and give it as much attention as you would, say, an expensive bike. Treat the bodywork – teeth, eyes, skin, hair – well!

4. Don't just sit there – remember our bodies were made for movement. Slump over a desk, or slouch

your sights on arriving. That's a roundabout way of saying that growing up can be a lot of fun if you set out to enjoy every minute.

Once upon a time growing was made to sound like a pretty gruesome business. Folk used to talk about 'growing pains'. These days doctors say that there is no physical pain attached to growing. The odd aches and pains in the legs and arms you may get when you're growing are usually more easily explained by you over-reaching yourself when it comes to exercise, or taking the usual playground/sports field knocks and bumps. They could even be caused by sitting the wrong way when you're studying so that your muscles feel the strain.

Obviously if you have any lasting or recurring discomfort in your limbs it isn't wise to simply dismiss it as 'growing pains'. You should always check it out with your parents and your doctor, though there's probably a simple reason for it.

For girls, of course, starting periods may occasionally cause a slight back or stomach ache – this can usually be helped with gentle exercise like walking (but nothing vigorous and no stomach-tightening movements).

We all go through lots of changes in the growing-up years, and as our bodies develop so do our personalities, interests and ideas. It's an exciting, though not always easy, time to live through. And super kids will set out to make the most of every minute.

around too long and your body will protest – it will ache, creak and begin to work less efficiently.

5. Walk tall. Good posture makes you look and feel better and even helps you think more clearly.

6. Get out into the great outdoors every day (even into the backgarden will do) for a fresh air booster – sunlight is the best source of vitamin D.

7. Be a good sport – remember that sports aren't just for those who are competitive. They're good for all of us, giving us better health, companionship, and team spirit – so even losers are winners!

8. Get plenty of sleep – it's Nature's refresher and growing bodies need plenty of it. Also learn to unwind and relax if you are worried or tense.

9. Be positive about yourself. Don't dwell on the things you dislike about the way you look, but concentrate on your good (no super!) qualities.

10. Banish boredom – nothing drains energy faster. There are millions of interesting things for super girls to do! Go out and enjoy 'em!